ONE WOMAN'S HEART

A collection of poems

By

Bonnie Lee Tatum

This book is a work of fiction. Places, events, and situations in this story are purely fictional. Any resemblance to actual persons, living or dead, is coincidental.

ISBN: 1-4033-0650-8

This book is printed on acid free paper.

1st Books - rev. 05/31/02

Dedication

This book would not be complete without giving my heartfelt words of thanks and gratitude. First, I thank God for the gift of words that He has given to me. It is my hope that His gift, through me, may bless another's heart.

I would like to thank my husband, Garry, for being my source of strength, my life's companion, and my best friend for many years. Our life together has inspired so much in me and has helped to create this woman's heart.

I would like to thank my children, Brandie and Michael, for filling my heart with more love and joy than I ever dreamed was possible. Their laughter, their smiles, and their happiness have been my driving force.

A special word of thanks goes to Dave "Tedd" Allen, Marie "Goofy" Haynes, Linda "Snick" Lewis and especially John "Uncle Bumpkin" Britt, for having the "whacky" idea that my poems should be published. Without the help, guidance, support and encouragement from these special friends, this book, and my dream would not have happened.

And finally, this book is dedicated to all those who have inspired me, believed in me, and who caused me to look inside my own heart to bring out the best in me. It is especially dedicated to my mother, Eva Grace Dunn.

CONTENTS

ON LOVE 37

ON FRIENDSHIP 49

ON LIFE 65

ON HEROES

ON

FAITH

Bonnie Lee Tatum

THE GIFT

What meaning is there to a life
When it's burdened down by daily
strife

What pleasure can one's soul know
When the spirit is not allowed to
grow

What worth is there to a being
When our calling goes without our
seeing

What disservice are we doing
When our dreams we're not
pursuing

To use the talents that God has
given
Is what makes a life on earth worth
livin'

One Woman's Heart

So on our knees our prayers we lift
And thank our Father for the gift

Bonnie Lee Tatum

GOD STEPS IN

Sometimes we face a burden
That seems too hard to bear
We walk around with our head held
down
Wondering if anyone cares

Sometimes all of the worries
Seem to mount up to the skies
We feel so down and discouraged that
We can't look others in the eyes

Our hearts are heavy and pulled low
It's almost hard to breathe
Our minds twist to find the answers
So that our souls can be at ease

But there comes a time when fighting
Must be given in to defeat
Just let the world swallow you up
Pull back, abort, retreat

That's when God steps in and takes over
He puts His hand in mine
And says, "Give me your troubles"
And I do....one teardrop at a time.

I Prayed

As I gazed upon the mountains
They seemed to beckon me today
So I sat quietly at their foothills
And I began to pray

I prayed for all dear children
Those both far and near
That they might know God's peace
tonight
And sleep without worry or fear

I prayed for those I love
That now rest in God's embrace
And took comfort in the knowledge

That they're in a better place

I prayed for all world leaders
That their decisions would be wise
And that what they are led to do
Would be noble in God's eyes

I prayed for my own family
That I would do my best
To be what God has called me to be
And that I would pass this test

I prayed for friendships present
And for those that have faded away
For memories and words unspoken
And words that got in the way

And I prayed for all tomorrows

Full of doubts and things unknown
That God's strength would support us
When to us these things are shown

Bonnie Lee Tatum

Come On Home

How insignificant our life seems
When we stand amidst our shattered dreams

Our hopes and dreams for a bright tomorrow
Have faded with today's own sorrow

Our hopes of working and giving care
Disappear like stars into thin air

What weight of purpose does life hold
Surrounded by a world that's cold

But to live for life beyond the skies
Where no one ever hurts or dies

No more hunger, no more pain
A place for our faith to regain

Our meager chores on earth foretell
The glories when we will dwell

In Heaven's gates some yonder day

And hear our Lord to us say

We've given everything we could
To make our life and world so good

The reason for our life has been
To turn ourselves and others from sin

What we have is precious and dear
But we only can have it here

Someday all things we know will be gone
That's when we'll sing a different song

Lying in a field we'll rest
And there we'll truly be well blessed

But for now we try to understand
While holding tightly to the Master's hand

Until the days of worry are gone
And God Himself says, "Come on home."

Bonnie Lee Tatum

Reunion at Heaven's Gate

As the cows and sheep bowed their heads,
Fulfillment was made to what the prophets
said.

With stars above shining so bright,
A little child was born that night.

Taken straight from God's embrace,
To live among the human race.

To give us hope in time of despair,
To cast on Him our every care.

To wipe away our every tear,
And stand with us through every fear.

This child was given in perfect love,
To give us grace from God above.

His time on earth was a short while,
To cause our hearts and souls to smile.

And from our sight now He is gone,
Back to His celestial home.

To walk where the angels trod,
And sit beside His Father God.

From where He sits upon His throne,
He calls His perfect children home.

Into His care we humbly trust,
When letting go becomes a must.

And now in sorrow we must wait,
Until our reunion at Heaven's gate.

Eva Grace Dunn

Eva Grace Dunn is my mother. She devoted her life to her family and worked hard to instill in us the principles of faith and family. Always there to lend a helping hand or a listening ear, she was my support, my encourager, and my best friend. She died December 20, 1998, and she is deeply missed.

He's Standing by Me

As I struggle through my daily life
Being someone's mother and someone's
wife
Trying to make this family's life
complete

Chasing rainbows that never end
Dodging bullets coming at me again
But I know….He's standing by me

Through the rainy days and the cloudless
skies
Through the long cold winters and the
sleepless nights
I know….He's standing by me

In my childhood days and in my adult
ways
Through the years of sin He's brought me
home again
And I know….He's standing by me

I don't know what tomorrow will bring
I might be crying or I might be singing

Bonnie Lee Tatum

So I'll let the bells of today ring loud and free

I could lose all that I now own
Everything in my life be gone
But I know....He'll be standing by me

Through the rainy days and the cloudless skies
Through the long cold winters and the sleepless nights
I know....He's standing by me

In my childhood days and in my adult ways
Through the years of sin He's brought me home again
And I know....He's standing by me

ROCK ME LIKE A BABY

Rock me like a baby
Hold me like a child
Keep me safe from evil
For I am meek and mild

Shed your love around me
And comfort me tonight
And with the faith of Jesus
I'll make it through the night

I am tired and lonely
I've struggled all the day
When I looked toward Heaven
My tears got in the way

You're the only person
Who can really understand
I'm reaching up to Heaven, Lord
Please take me by the hand

Bonnie Lee Tatum

ON

FAMILY

Michael & Brandie

MOTHERHOOD

Downy hair like an angel's wing
A cherub face against my breast
A lullaby I softly sing
While your body I caress

Your tiny eyes and little lips
Small fingers, ears, and toes

Into dreamland you quietly slip
Oh how my love for you grows

The softness of your newborn skin
The smell of you, so sweet
This is where motherhood begins
And what has made my life complete

Bonnie Lee Tatum

Brandie's Poem

I opened the trunk
In the attic of my mind
Blew the dust off the memories
And let the past rewind

A little girl in pigtails
Playing on the swing
Picking daffodils for Mommy
In the early days of spring

How your smile brought the sunshine
Your laughter chased away rain
Your eyes were full of wonder
Your voice like a sweet refrain

From "push me high as the sky"
To singing "I had a bird"
How I captured every moment
And hung on every word

From pageant days to softball
Pink dresses trimmed in lace
We traded your tiaras
For a glove and first base

Your handprints adorned the hallway
As did artwork made at school
In third grade I was your best friend
And you wrote how I was "so cool"

Sleepovers and girlfriends

Bonnie Lee Tatum

Talking on the line
I slowly took the backseat
But really, I didn't mind

For a mother knows deep down
That she must soon let go
To the little girl she's watched grow up
Even if it hurts her so

So as you take another step
Before time slips away
There's something that you need to know
Something I need to say

Though you may get older
And from my lap and arms depart
You'll always be my little girl
Deep down inside my heart

MICHAEL'S POEM

How was I to know
The joy that was to come
When I held you in my arms back then
My little boy...my son

Bonnie Lee Tatum

You came with such wonderment
Your curiosity knew no bounds
I knew you were up to something
When I couldn't hear you making sounds

You were quick as lightning
Darting to and fro
Never still for a moment
Always on the go

The falls, the spills, the boo-boos
Scraped and skinned up knees
I couldn't keep you from running
Or climbing high into the trees

Your curly hair, your bright blue eyes
Mischief in every smile

How I long to relive those days
And visit them once in a while

You taught me how to enjoy life
How to slow down and take time to play
You always could make me laugh
And chase my blues away

Some day you'll be a grown man
And your heart will belong to another
But you will always be a little boy
In this heart of mine... your mother

Bonnie Lee Tatum

Through A Child's Eyes

You gasped with shock,
And shook your head,
Then turned the TV off,

Your face was pale,
Your mouth agape,
You said, "Oh my gosh!"

"The words that they
Are using
Is language you shouldn't hear!"

I left the room,
My head hung low,
And wiped away a tear.

'Cause just last night
I heard you say
Words far worse than those,

When you looked under
The bed in my room
And found some dirty clothes.

You scolded me

The day that I
Hit a boy at school,

"Fighting is not allowed
In this house!
That is a rule!"

But you didn't know that I
Saw you slap Mommy
The other night,

When the two of you
Were having
Another one of your fights.

When it comes to friends,
I'm so confused,
I don't know what to do!

I want to play
With everyone,
Blacks, browns, and whites, too.

But I hear the things
You say about
People not like us,

So I don't play with them,

Or sit next to them,
At school or on the bus.

You supported Red Ribbon Week
And said that drugs
Are a mistake,

But I know what you've been doing
On the nights
You come home late.

You want to give me everything,
Or at least
What is ample,

But Mom and Dad
What I could use
Is a better "good example".

Sometimes when I do wrong,
You need to be
More forgiving,

'Cause I'm the one
Who is learning
From the way that you are living.

Clylia Lenora Cloer

This sweet lady is my grandmother, Clylia Lenora Cloer, or Sue Mama as she was known to all. It was a joy to visit her. She always had peanut butter cookies warm from the oven and a supply of "bottled cokes" for us kids. There's no doubt in my mind that she is in Heaven right now humming a hymn.

The poem "Mama Picking Pretty Flowers" was originally written as a song for my mother (Eva Grace Dunn) when her mother died (Clylia Lenora Cloer). Now as I read these words again, they are so very fitting to have been meant for either of these two ladies. This is a picture of me at age three sitting among "Sue Mama's" flowers.

Mama Picking Pretty Flowers

Mama loved to work out in her garden
Planting flowers for everyone to see
She had some sitting on the table
And a rose she always saved for me

And I'd see Mama picking pretty flowers
Then she'd kneel and bow her head to pray
She worked hard to make a pretty garden
She'd just smile and wipe the sweat away

When the Master called her to be His
gardener
He picked a rose to sit beside His throne
The flowers sent were all so very pretty
But not one as pretty as her own

I know that Mama's picking pretty flowers
In a garden up in Glory Land
She is smelling roses of scarlet
Planted by the Lord's own loving hand

And some day when harvest time has ended
And the Master reaps those that He has
sown

I'll see angels singing up in Glory
And meet those on earth that I have known

And I'll see Mama picking pretty flowers
In a garden as fair as eyes have seen
She'll be handing out daisies and lilies
But a rose I know she'll save for me

Granny's Kitchen

Granny's kitchen
Was a heavenly place
There was always a smile
Upon her face

The smell of cookies
Filled the air
Her childhood memories
She liked to share

Seeing her standing
Beside the sink
A glass of lemonade
Always to drink

Homemade biscuits
With syrup and butter
She was one of a kind
Unlike any other

Oh how I wish
That I could stay
In Granny's kitchen
Just one more day

Taking in
The sights and sounds
But especially the love
That knew no bounds

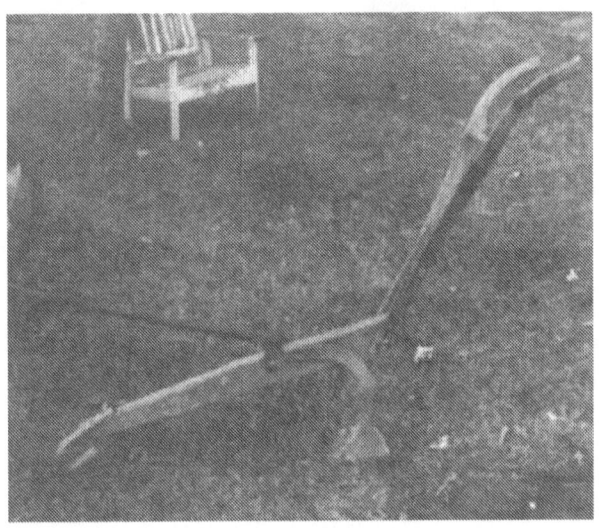

Plowin' Fields

Plowin' these fields in the hot summer sun
The sweat pourin' from my brow
Workin' all day to get the job done
Just my ol' mule and my plow

Plantin' them rows by the acreage
Earnin' a hard day's pay
Life in these farmlands is sacred
Workin' to survive another day

A hearty supper in the evenin'
A thanks to the good Lord above

35

My faith keeps me believin'
I work each day out of love

This hard work ain't gonna kill me
But one day, I'll lay this field by
'Neath the ground is where my body'll be
But I'll be plowin' fields in the sky

ON

LOVE

Garry & Bonnie Tatum

*Married September 6, 1981, these
high school sweethearts have spent
more than twenty years together*

building a company, a home, and a family. "God Gave Me You" was written in celebration of their sixteenth wedding anniversary.

Bonnie Lee Tatum

God Gave Me You

God knew I needed guidance
When decisions were hard to make
God gave me you.

God knew I needed to laugh
When there would be nothing to laugh about
God gave me you.

God knew I needed someone to hold me when I
cried
Even if the tears were all on the inside
God gave me you.

God knew I needed stability
When my head was in the clouds
God gave me you.

God knew I needed answers
Even when I wasn't sure what the questions
were
God gave me you.

God knew I needed a purpose for my life
So each day would be worth living
God gave me you.

God knew I needed someone to love me as
much as He does
And someone to love in return as much as I
love Him
God gave me you.

Bonnie Lee Tatum

SOMEBODY

Somebody cares for you
More than you know
Warm thoughts are with you
Wherever you go

Somebody wishes
The gray clouds away
Somebody hopes
That it's sunny each day

Somebody says
A little prayer too
That only the best things
Will happen to you

Whether together
Or miles far apart
You always are close

To that somebody's heart

And all through the years
That's the way it will be
Somebody loves you
And that somebody's me

Bonnie Lee Tatum

OUR LOVE

Our love is like a river
That flows on to the sea

Our love is like the seasons
That go on endlessly

Our love is like the morning sun
That warms the cold, dark night

Our love is what we've been
searching for
That makes us feel so right

Our love is like the bluebirds
That fly high as the pines

Our love is like the gray clouds
That are always sliver lined

Our love will shine forever
Because that's the way it should be

Our love could be a wondrous thing
If only you belonged to me

Bonnie Lee Tatum

Without the Love from You

While I watch the lights twinkle
And the stars that shine so bright
My heart is outside in the cold
My mind is in the night

I think of how it used to be
When time for us stood still
I wish of going back in time
And know I never will

I dream of midnight by the fire
Lying close to stay warm
Sharing our love beside the Christmas tree
Until the night turned into dawn

We didn't need a lot of presents
We had our love to see us through
Now our love is over
It wasn't enough for me and you

The Christmas tree stands empty
And I beside it, too
For Christmas isn't Christmas
Without the love from you

In My Dreams

I'll see you in my dreams tonight
The way I always do
I'll hug my pillow very tight
And make-believe its you

I'll whisper secrets in your ear
That only sweethearts share
I'll see you in my dreams tonight
And please, oh please, be there.

Bonnie Lee Tatum

The Words
of My Heart

My heart is like an open book
When it comes to you
You read each page so vividly
You read me through and through

You sense so much on the pages
Even more than I can see
You fill the empty spaces
To complete the book of me

You are my illustrations
You have been from the start
You are my life's author
You wrote the words of my heart

ON

FRIENDSHIP

Bonnie Lee Tatum

OUR FRIEND

God is never too busy
To hear or to answer our
prayers
He never holds back His
blessings
He always shows us how much
He cares

He is always there to listen
To lighten the load that we
hold
He always sends the sunshine
To warm us when the days are
cold

But He in His infinite wisdom
Knows how the human heart
can be

There are times a voice needs
to be heard
Times when a face we need to
see

So He sends to us a companion
Someone in whom we can
confide
Someone we can sit quietly
with
Or walk boldly side by side

Someone that is always near
One who never will depart
Someone to be close by us
Someone we keep inside our
heart

Someone whose face brightens
our days

Bonnie Lee Tatum

Whose smile takes us through
the night
Someone who lends a listening
ear
When things aren't going just
right

A friendly word, a kind deed
A soft and gentle touch
God knew we needed someone
like this
When life gets a little too much

So He sent to us someone
On whom we can depend
He calls them our angels
We simply call them our friend

My Best Friend

It was chance that birthed our
friendship
A fate we know not of
A kindred spirit bonded
Two hearts were bound by love

Side by side we face each day
Shouldering the other's care
Never alone or neglected
Knowing the other is there

No matter where the road may take
us
What lies ahead for me and you
Our friendship will endure it
Best friends....tried and true.

Bonnie Lee Tatum

GOD KNEW

God knew that I would need

A shoulder on which to lean

He knew that I couldn't dry

All the tears that fill my eyes

He knew there would be days

When I'd stumble along the

way

He knew I'd need a hug

And someone to pick me up

A soft voice, a kind word said

A strong shoulder where I

could rest my head

He knew sometimes my heart

would ache

To the point that I could feel it

break

He knew that when I'm feeling

down

When the world crashes all

around

On days when life seems so

unfair

He sent you, my friend, to be

there

Bonnie Lee Tatum

I THANK GOD

In the stillness of the night
When the stars are shining bright
And the moon casts down its light
I thank God that you're my friend

When the flowers are in bloom
And I can smell their sweet
perfume
Or during winter's bitter gloom
I thank God that you're my friend

When the world has turned away
When I can't face another day
By my side you're here to stay
I thank God that you're my friend

On those days when I am down
When no one cares to come around
And my heartbeat is the only
sound
I thank God that you're my friend

On the days when life's a pleasure
When blessings flow beyond
measure
You are my dearest treasure
I thank God that you're my friend

You bring the sunshine to my days
You give me more than words can
say
I love you in so many ways
I thank God that you're my friend

Side by side we'll always be
The best of buddies, you and me
I want the whole world to see
That I thank God that you're my
friend

Bonnie Lee Tatum

TOGETHER, ME AND YOU

It was raining when I met you
Some days it rains still
It seems that one of us is always
Climbing up another hill

That which bound us together
Draws us closer now again
But we will make it though it
Together, somehow, my friend

I'll ease your pain as best I can
I know that you'll ease mine
We'll hold tightly to our friendship
And take it one day at a time

I guess you can tell I'm hurting
You've seen me like this before
And you know in the days to come
I'll be like this even more

And so will you, I know
I'll hear it in your voice
I'll read it in a letter
But to me there'll be no choice

I'll give you words of comfort
And shoulders on which to cry
I can't make it any better
But you know that I will try

Sorrow brought us together
As the duo that we are
But love and friendship will keep us
Close in each other's hearts

Take these words as my gift
For the gift you've given to me
Know that you've been more
Than a friend could ever be

And on days when sadness fills me
And I think that no one cares
That's the day I'll take a look
And see you standing there

Because you always know my feelings
And you know just what to do
And I hope that when it's needed
I'll do the same for you

Here's to you, my little gal
And the friendship that we share
To knowing someone is there to listen
And knowing that someone cares

I thank God in His wisdom
When He took away our mothers
That He was merciful enough to us
That He gave to us each other

It's gonna be a hard time
But together we'll see it through
Day by day, never alone
Together, me and you

Linda Lee Lewis & Bonnie Lee Tatum met and became friends after the death of their mothers.

Bonnie Lee Tatum

GOIN FISHIN
(My Little Ol' Buddy and Me)

Sitting on the bank
Of our favorite fishin hole,
We've got our tackle, got our bait,
Got our line and pole.
Gonna wet our hooks till the sun goes
down
Behind the tall pine tree,
Just fishin away our worries....
My little ol' buddy and me.

Gonna rest our backs on the big tree's
trunk
And talk the day away,
We don't care if we catch a thing,
We'll have a good time anyway.

Jerkin our line when the red float sinks
'Neath that water's top,
Gonna laugh, we might even cry,
But the fun ain't gonna stop.

There's no better way to spend the day
'Cause we've tried it all, you see,
Gonna spend the day down at the fishin
hole,
Just my little ol' buddy and me.

ON

LIFE

Bonnie Lee Tatum

ONE DAY MORE

We never know our fate in life
From the moment of our birth
We know not the roads we'll travel
While walking upon this earth

The tears we'll cry, the pain we'll
bear
Is kept unknown to us
We wake each day to face the
world
Living in faith and trust

Our shattered dreams, our
adversities,
Things beyond our own control
Can wear us down from day to day
The worries can take their toll

If we were given just one chance
To see what our future holds
Would it weaken us beyond belief

Or make us strong and bold?

But which among us could deny
If we knew what lies in store
That we would be willing to accept
And to ask for one day more

Bonnie Lee Tatum

TIME'S SEA

Time's been a friend and an enemy
But time is all that I've got
Dreaming of things that I long for
Reminded of things I have not

Waiting each day for the answers
To questions that seem never to end
Keeping my spirits raised like a ship's sails
On an ocean being led by the wind

I sail each day on her waters
Floating on whitecaps of foam
Letting her current take me farther
Till one day the tide brings me home

I rock and I sway with her angry gales
And peacefully rest when she's calm
Soaking up sunshine and salt air
Healing my soul like a balm

I'll sail time's sea like a pirate
Life from her crow's nest I'll view
And someday when this voyage has ended
I'll anchor myself where dreams do come
true

Bonnie Lee Tatum

A Vision of Sunset

Casting my eyes toward the evening sky
I find what I've been searching for
An answered prayer I can't deny
A vision of Heaven's shore

The clouds display their colors true
So rich and bold and bright
Drawing upon every hue
To light up the sky this night

The day is fading into dusk
My prayers go up once more

Retaining this vision is a must
It's what I've been searching for

Bonnie Lee Tatum

A Single Flame

Where does a poet find the words
A composer, the melody
To release their inspiration
For all the world to see

What does the sculptor feel
When his hands are on the clay
Or the artist with his canvas
His vision a brush stroke away

The actor upon the stage
Bringing a story to life
The viewer feels his happiness
Or his pain and strife

What is it within them
That entices us so
It is but a single flame
And it's illuminating glow

No greater sorrow has been known
When the shadows of fear and doubt
Are allowed to suppress that flame
And it puts the fire out

GOING FORWARD

You can't take one step forward
When your eyes are looking back
You can't be thankful for what you have
When you long for what you lack

You can't see the morning sunshine
While chasing nightmares in the dark
You can't keep a fire burning
When you're putting out each spark

See each day as being golden
Love your fellowman
Kiss a newborn baby
Take a child by the hand

Don't waste your time wishing
For the things for which you long
One day you may awaken
And find what you needed most is gone

Our trials are only temporary
And our tears are but a few
But the love you share is priceless
And it will flow right back to you

So sing yourself a new song

Bonnie Lee Tatum

And dream your dreams again
Cherish the blessings of today
For tomorrow could be the end

Letting Go

Standing on the very edge
Of a rocky mountainside
Watching the eagles as they soar
How effortlessly they glide

Sailing on the winds of time
Their power is released
They soar through life's adversities
They've found their perfect peace

What is their secret?
What is it that they know?
They dare to take a chance
They risk it all... and they let go

Bonnie Lee Tatum

THE MIRROR

Gaze into the mirror,
What is it that you find?
Is it the person that you've become,
Or the one you left behind?

Do you see the child inside,
Hope dancing in his eyes?
Or do you see a weary man,
Too tired even to cry?

Do you see a fallen star,
With its light burned out?
Do you carry upon your face,
Years of worries and doubt?

Maybe it's not the mirror,
That reflects what is not you.
Maybe it's the eyes,
That you are looking through.

SEARCHING FOR MY HOME

While in darkness yet I wander
Searching for my home
Questions unanswered I ponder
Traveling down this road alone

Seeking for life's contentment
Knowing not which path to take
Holding onto past resentment
Pained by memories I cannot shake

Feeling years of doubt and worry
Weighing greatly upon my chest
Scarcely outrunning the hurry
Never seeming to have rest

Looking back and not denying
Wasted hours of one's self
Speaking still, but yet am lying
Dreams stacked high upon a shelf

Yet in the years ahead I wonder
If any more to be will come
Unanswered questions still to
ponder
Will I finally find my home

Bonnie Lee Tatum

A SAVING PULL

Demons steal away your dreams

Only shadows can hear your silent

screams

You're a faceless being amid the crowd

There's only a whisper when you cry out

loud

Hope is drowned in a raging sea

Your soul is longing to be set free

The bridge ahead has been washed away

You fight to survive another day

Your heart sinks heavily inside

Your darkest fears you cannot hide

Your mind is scarred from endless

thinking

You struggle to hold on, but continue

sinking

A plea of rescue you shout

A saving pull from the river of doubt

From one who is so much stronger

And you hold on, a little longer

Bonnie Lee Tatum

Well Done

When the storm clouds have passed
And the day's given way to night
That's when my heart is at peace
And I know everything's going to be
alright

When the worries of the day are over
And I know I've done my best
That's when my mind is at ease
And that's when my soul is at rest

I've battled the day like a soldier
I've fought every battle, and won
I lie in solemn gratification
Victorious in a job well done.

Our Own Rainbow

We look through the clouds that cover
our souls
Trying to catch a glimpse of the sun
Searching for answers to conquer our
goals
Concluding within that there's none

Dodging the raindrops like bullets
As tears down our face do fall
Climbing yet another mountain's summit
Crashing against another wall

Smiles slowly fade like the embers
Of the fire that has lost its glow
Searching within to remember
The joy of a colorful rainbow

Its colors stretch across the sky
So vivid and yet so surreal
The beauty of it catches our eye
Its promise of hope we can feel

For we know that in life it's a given
We need the rain to make the flowers
grow
So we keep going on believin'
Until we find our own rainbow

Emotionally Tired

My inner strength has given up on what I'd like
to be
It seems I can't do anything right, or so it
seems to me

I'm tired of trying to live up to the woman in my
head
Spending another day with her is something that
I dread

She thinks that I should be somehow a super
kind of being
But I fall short of her ideals according to what
I'm seeing

She wears so many hats and does so many things
with flair
To match my skills against her own, well they
don't compare

I wish that she would let me be, leave me alone
for a while
Keeping up with her is taking away my laughter
and my smile

But, she nudges me on, another day in which to
deal

With all of life's "little things"...no matter how I
feel

So in my melancholy mood somehow I became
inspired
To jot down this little note.... I'm just emotionally
tired

ON

SEASONS

Bonnie Lee Tatum

MOTHER EARTH

There's a stirring inside Mother Earth
Her secrets she longs to reveal
Springtime within her has awakened
Winter's frostiness she'll steal

Her flowers emerge from their sepulcher
Her trees are beginning to bloom
There's a blanket of grass to cover her
Woven upon her own loom

The intoxicating fragrance of springtime
Hangs heavily upon the air
The subtle, gentle showers
Wash away every care

This is a time of hope and wonder
A time for growth and rebirth
A time to reap the blessings
Of majestic Mother Earth

COME, SWEET AUTUMN

Come, Sweet Autumn, come
Paint with your brush for me
The colors of your beauty
For all the world to see

The landscape is your canvas
Your palette's filled with hue
Transformation is your handiwork
The model used is you

Your hair's a brilliant golden
Gently kissed by nature's breeze
Your eyes a deepened amber
Twinkling while you tease

Burgundy cheeks rise highly
Above lips of scarlet red
Soft bronze skin adorns you
An orange halo surrounds your
head

Bonnie Lee Tatum

Come, Sweet Autumn, I implore
Your audience awaits
To view the artist as she works
The masterpiece she creates

AUTUMN

Autumn knocks with her chilly breeze,
Stirring up memories in fall's colored
leaves.

Shadows hang like a watchful eye,
And darkness comes sooner in the cold
night's sky.

The pumpkins are waiting their faces to
bear,
Children play joyfully without ever a
care.

Hay bales stacked high and their scent oh
so sweet,
Apples for drying, for baking, to eat.

Sweaters emerge from their summer's
prison,
You can hear time slowing down if only
you'd listen.

Bonnie Lee Tatum

Wrapped in the arms of autumn's
embrace,
The North Georgia Mountains, there's no
better place.

WINTER'S WONDERLAND

Heaven's skies are consumed by
winter's bitter chill,
Her secrets no longer can she contain.
Her arms burst open, her treasures to
spill,
The snowflakes fall like rain.

Peacefully falling into the sky,
They float like whispers on air.
Riding the wind they gracefully fly,
White ladies dancing so fair.

Lighting on earth these fairies fall,
Like a lover's kiss upon your face.
Quietly touching the child in us all,
Winter's wonderland we embrace.

Bonnie Lee Tatum

WINTER'S HERE

Gather 'round, I'll tell the story,
That winter's here in all her glory.

Electric blankets upon the bed,
Warm coats and hats upon your head.

Chilly nights to cuddle close,
Frosty winds nip at your nose.

Christmas plays and "Deck the Halls",
Crowded stores and shopping malls.

Turkey feasts and pumpkin pies,
Hopes of Santa in little eyes.

Stockings hung and lights all aglow,
One more present left to go.

Memories of yesteryear,
Joys, smiles, and a few tears.

Snow is predicted in the forecast,
Winter is here, again, at last.

School will be closed for a day or so,

Lord help the mommies during the snow.

Ice hangs thick on the Georgia pines,
Hanging from rooftops and power lines.

Winter comes but once each year.
It's time again, winter's here.

Bonnie Lee Tatum

ON

HOLIDAYS

Bonnie Lee Tatum

DON'T WAIT

The turkey has roasted nice and brown
The kitchen smells of pumpkin pies
Family and friends are gathered around
But I wonder if they realize...

The table is covered from end to end
With a feast beyond compare
Anticipation does transcend
But I wonder if they are aware...

With tummies full and waistbands tight
Leftovers are put away
It's time to tell them all good night
But I wonder, did they stop and say...

Thank you to God above
For bringing them together
Thanking Him for the love
That will live and grow forever

Did they tell the ones that they love
What happiness and joy they spread
Were the words that they were thinking of
Spoken, or left unsaid

Did they stop to think that tomorrow
All of this could be no more
Sickness, pain, death and sorrow
Could be waiting at the door

On this day of Thanksgiving
Say the things that should not wait

Rejoice in blessings and in living
For tomorrow may be too late

Bonnie Lee Tatum

Light of Christmas

It started with a single star
Shining in the sky that night
A star unlike the others
A star more brilliant and bright

Shepherds saw its wonder
While devotedly tending their sheep
They traveled onward to the place
Where the babe lay fast asleep

The wise men saw it from afar
To Him their gifts did bring
The angels filled the midnight sky
Their chorus of praise to sing

A young girl became a mother
Her innocence so pure
Not knowing such atrocities
Her babe would soon endure

A humble man of carpentry

Loved Him as his own
Willing to let others wonder
Taking the rocks that were thrown

The hope of all tomorrow
Was born upon that eve
The gift of all eternity
For those who would believe

A single star from Heaven
Became a baby in the hay
The light of Him continues
And guides us through each day

So at this Christmas season
Don't forget to take the time
To open your heart to that baby
And through you, let His light shine

Bonnie Lee Tatum

YOU'LL NEVER SEE CHRISTMAS

You'll never see Christmas
Its wonder and joy
Until you see it through
Eyes of a little girl or boy

You'll never see Christmas
In all of its glory
Until you see it through
The true Christmas story

You'll never see Christmas
The giving and sharing
Until you see it with
A friend that is caring

You'll never see Christmas
At an unhurried pace
Until you see it on
A grandfather's face

You'll never see Christmas
The way it was meant
Unless you live it each day
In hours well spent

You'll never see Christmas
What it's really made of
Until you see it through
A heart filled with love

Bonnie Lee Tatum

THE CHRISTMAS SPIRIT

Where is the Christmas spirit
That I knew when I was young?
Is it in the decorations,
Or in the carols that are sung?

Is it hiding in the presents
Underneath the Christmas tree?
Oh Christmas spirit where are you?
Where could you possibly be?

Is it someplace I'm not looking,
Someplace that I've forgot?
Could it be that it's right here with me,
Somewhere deep inside my heart?

The Christmas spirit does not hang
Within the light strands across the roof.
The Christmas spirit won't be found
With the prancing of each little hoof.

It won't be seen in the candles,
Their flames burning low.

It won't be felt by the fireside,
The embers all aglow.

There's only one place you'll find it,
Only one place it can hide,
Stop looking for it outwardly,
'Cause it's hidden deep inside.

If you want to feel the Christmas spirit,
To see what others are speaking of,
Then take a look inside yourself,
And fill your heart with love.

For Christmas means nothing
Without our love to share,
It's in the giving and kindness,
It's in the gentleness and care.

It's in loving your fellowman,
Treating everyone like a sister or
brother.
It's giving a little of yourself,
To make things easier for another.

So love and give and share yourself,
For it's no good until you give it.
And when you've done this until it hurts,

Bonnie Lee Tatum

That's when you'll find the Christmas spirit.

IT'S CHRISTMASTIME AGAIN

Don't want to hear the Christmas carols
Sung by the choir,
All I want is to be with you
Nestled in close by the fire.

Don't want to wrap another present
Or place another bow,
All I want is to hear you say
That you still love me so.

Don't want to hang a shimmering
ornament
Or tinsel on the tree,
Your shining eyes are the only
Twinkling thing I want to see.

Don't care about candy canes,
Cookies, pies or cake,
If you're not here this Christmas
My heart will surely break.

The sadness, the sorrow,
The tears, when will it end?
Look around, want it or not,
It's Christmastime, again.

Bonnie Lee Tatum

CHRISTMAS MORN

Wake up sleepy heads
Let's walk across the floor
Don't make a sound
And we'll peep inside the door

There's big green tree
With presents underneath
And on your door
Is a little green wreath

There's gift for you and your brother
One to and from your father and mother
There's a gift for all, one for everyone
Its Christmas morning, and we're going to
have fun

ON

HEROES

Bonnie Lee Tatum

I NEVER KNEW YOUR NAME
(A tribute to our Veterans)

You kissed your mother's tear stained cheek
You shook your father's hand
You climbed aboard the carrier
That would take you to an unknown land

Fatigues became your daily wear
A fox hole became your home
You gave up all of your comforts
So that liberty could live on

You stood proudly upon that battlefield
Your comrades by your side
You faced the enemy fearlessly
Some of you lived, while others died

You gave everything that you could give
For the country that you love
So that we could all pursue
What our American dream is made of

You returned to us a changed man
Each with his own war story
Some came back broken and wounded

Others in a box draped by Old Glory

For strangers that you never knew
You sacrificed, you bled, you fought
What did we give to you in return?
Was there something that you sought?

After the parades and fanfare
After all was said and done
Was your soul satisfied with meaning?
Did you feel that we had become one?

For me you gave your everything
My freedoms remain the same
All I can say is, "Thank you, Vets"
Sadly, I never knew your name

Bonnie Lee Tatum

A Grown Man Cry

Have you been there when a grown man
cries?
Watch him wipe the tears from his eyes?
The anguish written upon his face,
As the memories he tries to erase.
The pain he tries so hard to hide,
When he remembers those who fought and
died.
The anger he feels deep in his soul,
When he hears one say, "No, I won't go."
To fight for the freedoms we all enjoy.
To preserve the liberties we all employ.
Recalling the names of those who bled,
Those that suffered, those now dead.
He hears the cries of those against war,
And wonders what it was all for.
When gratitude is not realized,
That's what makes a grown man cry.

Bonnie Lee Tatum

About the Author

Bonnie Lee Tatum was born and raised in the small town of Canton, Georgia. The daughter of loving parents and the youngest of five children, she began writing at the tender age of seven as a means to express her feelings. That first work was a reflection that she penned while sitting at a small, wooden school desk the day after her grandfather's death, and was published in the local newspaper.

She married her high school sweetheart, and together they have built not only a company and a partnership, but a family that includes their daughter and son. The bond of family, friendships, and a strong faith in God is the motivation behind her work, and her life. Putting her thoughts and sentiments onto paper is a release as well as a calling. Like an artist with a brush, she has a picturesque style of writing that brings each work to life.

At the persuasion of family and friends, she has taken a collection of her words and her works (that span three decades) and has compiled them into her dream come true. Within these pages you will catch a glimpse of her passion for life, her devotion to loved ones, and the hope that sees her through life's adversities. Within these pages lies the essence of *One Woman's Heart*.